You Are God's Masterpiece

ISBN 978-1-63844-982-9 (paperback)
ISBN 978-1-63844-983-6 (digital)

Christian Faith Publishing, Inc.
832 Park Avenue
Meadville, PA 16335
www.christianfaithpublishing.com

Printed in the United States of America

You Are God's Masterpiece

Amanda P. Evans

Illustrated by Lauren Paschal

HEY, you!

Yes, you!

Did you know you are a masterpiece?
Did you know you were created and
formed by a great, big God?

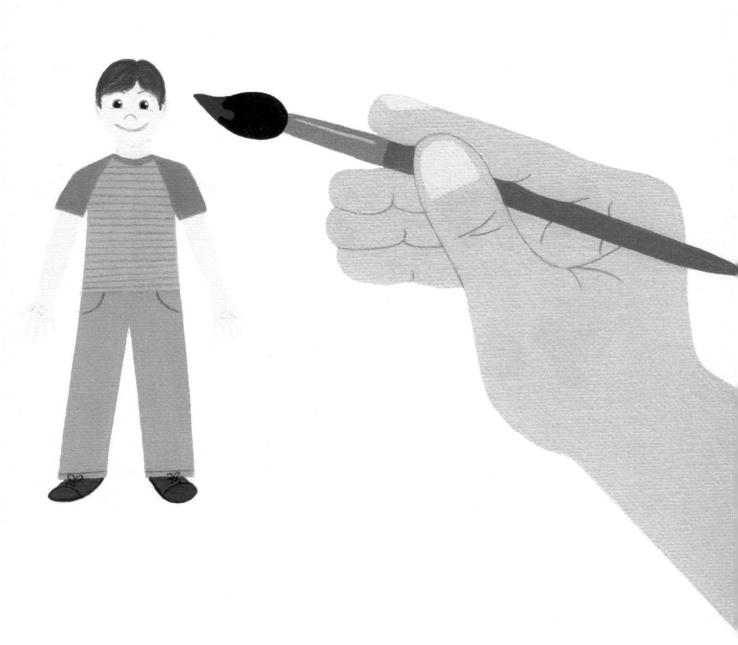

From your silly laugh to your wiggly toes
What you're destined to be, only He knows.

Do you have brown or green eyes? Hazel or blue?

Have you been here for a while,
or are you brand-new?

Is your hair long or short? Black,
brown, blonde, or red?
Does it flow down to the floor or
barely cover your head?

Are you tall or short?
Are you fast or slow?
Do you have listening ears
to help you as you go?

Do you have cute dimples? Is your skin light or dark?
Do you have freckles on your
cheeks or tiny beauty marks?

Do you like the taste of vegetables, like peas, carrots, and beets?

Or are cakes, lollipops, and ice cream your absolute favorite treats?

God's Art Gallery

There is only one you that has ever been.
And you are so special you make God grin!

He created your body to be just what He wanted it to be.
You are special in His eyes and the only you He will ever see.

You are a part of God's creation
that will never, ever cease.

You are beautiful,
and you are God's
Masterpiece!

Draw your self-portrait here!

13

About the Author

Amanda Evans grew up in a loving Christian family in the beautiful state of North Carolina, where she still makes her home today along with her husband, Derek, and their four children. She has served in education for over fourteen years, having taught in child-care settings, school-age classrooms, and is now currently serving as a private school principal. It has always been her dream to write stories and literature that would entertain, but more importantly, inspire children everywhere to recognize the unique gifts that they are to our world and how special they are to God.

CPSIA information can be obtained
at www.ICGtesting.com
Printed in the USA
BVHW020844270222
630162BV00016B/1032